Luke Holbrook in asso[c]
for the Finborough The[atre]

C000083564

The English Premiere

# SOMERSAULTS

by Iain Finlay Macleod

# FINBOROUGH | THEATRE

First commissioned and performed by the National Theatre of Scotland
at the Traverse Theatre, Edinburgh, on 10 March 2010

First performance at the Finborough Theatre: Wednesday, 2 January 2013

# SOMERSAULTS

by Iain Finlay Macleod

*Cast in order of appearance*

| | |
|---|---|
| James | **David Carlyle** |
| Mark | **Simon Harrison** |
| Alison | **Emily Bowker** |
| Barrett | **Richard Teverson** |
| Sandy | **Tom Marshall** |

The action takes place in London and on the Isle of Lewis in the present day.

The performance lasts approximately 90 minutes.

There will be no interval.

| | |
|---|---|
| Director | **Russell Bolam** |
| Designer | **Philip Lindley** |
| Lighting Designer | **Elliot Griggs** |
| Sound Designer | **Max Pappenheim** |
| Costume Designer | **Abigale Lewis** |
| Movement Director | **Jenny Ogilvie** |
| Production Manager | **David Leigh-Pemberton** |
| Casting Director | **Ruth O'Dowd** |
| Stage Manager | **Tim Berryman** |
| Assistant Director | **Stuart Burrows** |
| Producer | **Luke Holbrook** |
| Assistant Producer | **Saskia Lortz** |
| Marketing | **Katey Warran** |

**David Carlyle** | James
Trained at Rose Bruford College.
Theatre includes *Caledonia* (National Theatre of Scotland), *Yellow Moon* and *The Monster in the Hall* (National Theatre of Scotland and Citizens Theatre, Glasgow), *Hansel and Gretel* (Citizens Theatre, Glasgow), *Dead Heavy Fantastic* (Liverpool Everyman) and *You Once Said Yes* (Edinburgh Festival).
Theatre whilst training includes *The Wonderful World of Dissocia*, *Philistines*, *The White Devil*, *Hedda Gabler* and *Celebration/Party Time*. David also represented Rose Bruford College at the Sam Wanamaker Festival 2010 (Shakespeare's Globe).
Television includes *Lip Service II*.
Radio *Where Were You?, Chernobyl* and *Sudbury Hill*.

**Simon Harrison** | Mark
At the Finborough Theatre, Simon appeared in *Hortensia and The Museum Of Dreams* (2005).
Trained at the University of Hull and the London Academy of Music and Dramatic Art.
Theatre includes *Days of Significance* (Royal Shakespeare Company at the Tricycle Theatre and National Tour), *The Winter's Tale* and *Pericles* (Royal Shakespeare Company), *Journey's End* (National Tour and West End), *Bus* and *Twelfth Night* (West Yorkshire Playhouse), *Noises Off* and *Dr Faustus* (Liverpool Playhouse), *Relatively Speaking* and *The Importance of Being Earnest* (Library Theatre, Manchester), *The Picture* and *Private Lives* (Salisbury Playhouse), *The War on Terror* (Bush Theatre), *Look Back in Anger* (Jermyn Street Theatre), *Reclining Nude in Black Stockings* (Arcola Theatre), *They Have Oak Trees in North Carolina* (Theatre503), *The Conquering Hero* (Orange Tree Theatre, Richmond), *A Lie of The Mind*, *Feeding Time* (Battersea Arts Centre), *Epic* and *Merryweather Jones* (Latitude Festival), *A Midsummer Night's Dream* (Milton Rooms), *Penetrator* (Edinburgh Festival), *One Mile Away* (Spread the Word) and *A Devilish Exercise* (Rose Theatre, Bankside).
Television includes *Doctors*.
Radio includes *Idylls Of The King* and *They Have Oak Trees in North Carolina*.

**Emily Bowker** | Alison

At the Finborough Theatre, Emily appeared in *Too True to be Good* (2009).

Trained at Royal Welsh College of Music and Drama.

Theatre includes *Our Country's Good* (National Tour), *Daisy Pulls it Off* (National Tour), *Poor Cousin* (Hampstead Theatre), *Hay Fever* (West Yorkshire Playhouse), *250 Words* (The Young Vic), *The Importance of Being Earnest* and *Travesties* (Birmingham Rep), *Present Laughter* (Clwyd Theatr Cymru), *Antigone* (Bristol Old Vic), *Shakespeare and Co* (Watermill Theatre, Newbury, and Tour), *Mister Murdery* (Nuffield Theatre, Southampton), *A Bigger Banner* (Theatre Uncut at the Latitude Festival), *Devon Country* (The Tobacco Factory), *Births, Marriages and Deaths* (High-Hearted Theatre), *Great Undertaking in Little America* (Everyman Theatre, Cheltenham), *Look Back in Anger* and *A Midsummer Night's Dream* (Garrick Theatre, Lichfield), *Much Ado About Nothing* (Ripley Castle, Harrogate), *Noises Off* (Torch Theatre, Milford Haven), *Lie of the Land* (Arcola Theatre) and *Reunion* (Theatre503).

Film includes *Tezz* and *City Rats*.

Television includes *Upstairs Downstairs*, *Holby City*, *Torchwood*, *The Bill*, *Doctors*, *Shameless*, *Wire in the Blood* and *When Calls the Heart*.

Radio includes *High Table*, *Lower Orders*, *Swimming Lessons*, *Roundabout* and *Mortar*.

**Richard Teverson** | Barrett

Trained at the Webber Douglas Academy of Dramatic Art.

Theatre includes *The Doctor's Dilemma* (National Theatre), *Cause Célèbre* (The Old Vic), *After the Dance* (National Theatre), *The 39 Steps* (Criterion Theatre), *When Harry Met Sally* and *A Woman of No Importance* (Theatre Royal Haymarket), *The Lion King* (Lyceum Theatre), *Private Lives*, *Tons of Money*, *Hobson's Choice* (Southwold Theatre), *The Singing Group* (Chelsea Theatre), *Cleo, Camping, Emmanuelle and Dick* (New Vic Theatre, Staffordshire) and *A Midsummer Night's Dream* (Creation Theatre).

Film includes *Brideshead Revisited*, *Private Peaceful* and *Workhorse*.

Television includes *Downton Abbey*, *The Spies of Warsaw*, *Dancing On The Edge*, *Upstairs Downstairs*, *The Roman Mysteries*, *Live! Girls! Dogtown*, *Balderdash and Piffle*, *Poirot: Five Little Pigs* and *The Project*.

Radio includes *Noise* and *Cause Célèbre*.

Voiceover work includes many unabridged audiobooks and *Star Wars: The Old Republic*.

**Tom Marshall** | Sandy

At the Finborough Theatre, Tom appeared in *Captain Oates' Left Sock* (2009).

Trained at the London Academy of Music and Dramatic Art.

Theatre includes *Total Eclipse* (Menier Chocolate Factory), *The Anatomist* (Eastern Angles), *The Pillars of the Community, Henry IV, Parts I and II, Tales of the Vienna Woods, Edmond, Luther, The Spanish Tragedy, Antigone, Danton's Death,* and *Venice Preserv'd* (National Theatre), *Mandrake, Snap, No Man's Land, The Passion of Dracula, Plenty, Passion Play, When Did You Last See Your Trousers?* (all West End), *The Crucible* (Birmingham Rep), *Karate Billy Comes Home* (Royal Court Theatre), *Rosmersholm* (Southwark Playhouse), *Twelfth Night* (Perth Theatre), as well as repertory seasons at Glasgow, Lincoln, Canterbury, Bristol, Cardiff, Watford, Oxford, Edinburgh and Sheffield.

Film includes *Oh What a Lovely War!, There's a Girl in my Soup, Infinity, Revenge, Killer's Moon,* and *Feast of July.*

Television includes *Upstairs Downstairs, Please Sir, Doctor at Large, Coronation Street, Spooks, World's End, The Thin End of the Wedge, Juliet Bravo, Blind Justice, Joint Account, The Bill, Casualty, Mornin' Sarge, March on Europe,* and *The Paradise Club.*

**Iain Finlay Macleod** | Playwright

Playwright Iain Finlay Macleod made his English theatre debut at the Finborough Theatre in 2009 with *I Was A Beautiful Day* in a production which subsequently transferred to the Tron Theatre, Glasgow. His play *Atman* was also produced at the Finborough Theatre in 2011 starring Lucy Griffiths, following a staged reading as part of the Finborough Theatre's *Vibrant – A Festival of Finborough Playwrights* with Jasper Britton and Alan Cox.

Iain Finlay has written many works for theatre, radio, film and television. Writing in both English and his native Scots Gaelic, Iain has also directed numerous documentaries, and was series director of the BAFTA-winning show *TACSI*, which won Best Arts Series in the Scottish BAFTAs and Best Entertainment Programme at the Celtic Film and Television Festival. Television includes *Machair* which won a Writers' Guild Award for Best Foreign Language Serial Drama. His work for theatre includes *Somersaults* (National Theatre of Scotland), *St Kilda – The Opera*; a multi-discipline work performed simultaneously in five countries, *The Pearlfisher*, *Broke*, *Homers* and *Alexander Salamander* (Traverse Theatre), *Salvage* (Tosg Theatre Company). His work for BBC Radio 4 includes *Mr Anwar's Farewell to Stornoway*, *The Watergaw*, *The Gold Digger* and an adaptation of Angela Carter's *The Kitchen Child*. Other radio includes *Frozen* and an adaptation of *The Pearlfisher* for BBC Radio Scotland. His film work includes *Seachd: The Inaccessible Pinnacle*. He is also the author of several novels.

**Russell Bolam** | Director

At the Finborough Theatre, Russell directed the sell-out production of John Antrobus' *Captain Oates' Left Sock* (2009).

Trained at Middlesex University and GITIS Academy of Theatre Arts, Moscow. Directing includes *Shivered* which was nominated for four OffWestEnd awards including Best Director and for Best Production at the WhatsOnStage awards (Southwark Playhouse), *The Seagull* (Southwark Playhouse), *The Road to Mecca* (Arcola Theatre), *The Roman Bath* (Arcola Theatre and Ivan Vazov National Theatre), *Alfred* (Vineyard Theatre, New York, as part of the T.S. Eliot Exchange), *Lark Ascending* (Theatre503), *Three More Sleepless Nights* and *Fourplay* (Tristan Bates Theatre), *Fairytaleheart* (Old Red Lion Theatre) and *The Physicists* (The Aphra Studio, Canterbury). Assistant Directing includes *The Winter's Tale*, *Pericles*, *Days of Significance* (Royal Shakespeare Company Complete Works Season and US Tour), *An Inexplicable Act of Violence* (Old Vic 24 Hour Plays), *A Background Noise* (Nottingham Playhouse), *The Taming of the Shrew*, *Around the World in 80 Days*, *The Barber of Seville* and *The Seagull* (Bristol Old Vic).

**Philip Lindley** | Designer

At the Finborough Theatre, Philip is Associate Designer, and has designed *Mirror Teeth* (2011), *Drama At Inish* (2011), *Autumn Fire* (2012), *The American Clock* (2012), *Merrie England* (2012), *The Fear of Breathing* (2012) and *Passing By* (2012).

Trained as an architect, Philip began his theatre career as a set and lighting designer before joining the BBC TV Design Department. During 25 years at the BBC, he worked on every type of production including *Dr Who, Blackadder, Top Of The Pops, Mastermind, Swap Shop, Play For Today, Play For Tomorrow, 30 Minute Theatre, Lorna Doone, Z For Zacharias, The Tripods, Juliet Bravo, Rings On Their Fingers, The Kamikaze Ground Staff Dinner Party, Goodbye Darling, Tomorrow's World, The 1981 Royal Wedding* and *The Scientist.* After leaving the BBC, he worked as a freelance theatre consultant before moving to Lisbon where he continued to design sets and lighting for Portuguese theatre including productions of *Cymbeline, Saturday Sunday Monday, The Bear, The Proposal, Recklessness, Tone Clusters, One For The Road, A Time For Farewells, and Dracula.* He recently returned to live in the UK, and has since designed *Nerve, The Good Doctor* and *Sleeping Dogs* (Baron's Court Theatre), *Miss Julie* (Teatro Technis), *The Three Sisters* and *Endgame* (Bridewell Theatre).

**Elliot Griggs** | Lighting Designer

At the Finborough Theatre, Elliot has been the Lighting Designer for *The Soft of Her Palm* (2012), *Crush* (2011), *Perchance to Dream* (2011), *Portraits* (2011), *And I and Silence* (2011) and *Northern Star* (2011).

Trained at the Royal Academy of Dramatic Art. Recent theatre includes *The Boy Who Kicked Pigs* (The Lowry, Manchester), *MEAT* (Theatre503), *Belleville Rendez-Vous* (Greenwich Theatre), *Lagan* (Oval House Theatre), *Folk Contraption* (Southbank Centre), *Bitter Pleasures for a Sour Generation* (Soho Theatre), *Joe/Boy* (The Last Refuge), *Big Sean, Mikey and Me* (Tristan Bates Theatre), *The Custard Boys* (Tabard Theatre), *Brightest and Best* (Half Moon Theatre), *Dealing With Clair, One Minute, Nocturnal, Dirty Butterfly, Our Town* (Royal Academy of Dramatic Art), *The Mercy Seat* (Royal Shakespeare Company Capital Centre, Warwick), *The Lady's Not For Burning, West Side Story, By the Bog of Cats, 'Tis Pity She's a Whore, Elephant's Graveyard* (Warwick Arts Centre), *Much Ado About Nothing* (Belgrade Theatre, Coventry) and *Dido and Aeneas* (St. Paul's Church, London, and Tour). His awards for lighting design include the Francis Reid Award from the Association of Lighting Designers and the ShowLight Award at the National Student Drama Festival.

**Max Pappenheim** | Sound Designer
At the Finborough Theatre, Max designed the sound and original composition for *The Soft of Her Palm* (2012), *So Great A Crime* (2012), *The Fear of Breathing* (2012), *Barrow Hill* (2012) and *Hindle Wakes* (2012), and directed *Perchance to Dream* (2011) and *Nothing is the End of the World (Except the End of the World)* as part of *Vibrant 2012 – A Festival of Finborough Playwrights* (2012).
Sound Designs include *Borderland*, *Kafka v Kafka* (Brockley Jack Studio Theatre), *Being Tommy Cooper* (Old Red Lion Theatre), *Four Corners One Heart* (Theatre503) and *Tangent* (New Diorama Theatre). Directing includes *San Giuda* (Southwark Cathedral), *The Charmed Life* (King's Head Theatre), *Finchley Road* (LOST Theatre) and *Quid Pro Quo* (Riverside Studios). Max was nominated for an OffWestEnd Award 2012 for Best Sound Design.

**Abigale Lewis** | Costume Designer
Costume design includes *Baba Shakespeare* (Arcola Tent and Courtyard Theatre), *Endgame* and *Three Sisters* (Bridewell Theatre), *Miss Julie* (Theatro Technis). Abigale also works as a freelance costume dyer and as a dresser at the Royal Opera House. Recently worked as a dyer on *The Cunning Little Vixen*, *Le Nozze Di Figaro* and *the Ravel Double Bill* (Glyndebourne Opera House) and *Carmen* (English National Opera).

**Jenny Ogilvie** | Movement Director
At the Finborough Theatre, Jenny appeared as an actor in *Wolfboy/Treatment* (1999), *Beating Heart Cadaver* (2010) and *Pig Girl* (2012) as part of *Vibrant – A Festival of Finborough Playwrights*, and was Movement Director on *The Soft of Her Palm* (2012).
Trained as an actor at the Webber Douglas Academy of Dramatic Art and as a Movement Director at the Central School of Speech and Drama. Movement Direction includes *Sweeney Todd* and *Paul Bunyan* workshops (Welsh National Opera), *Vernon God Little* (Guildford School of Acting), *Three Sisters/Swan Song*, which she co-directed with Ben Naylor, *Richard III*, *Antony and Cleopatra* (Central School of Speech and Drama). As an actor, theatre includes *What Every Woman Knows* (Royal Exchange Theatre, Manchester), *Noughts and Crosses* (Royal Shakespeare Company), *I Have Been Here Before* (Watford Palace Theatre), *Peter Pan*, *The Diary of Anne Frank* (Birmingham Rep and National Tour), *Our Country's Good* (National Tour), *Rebecca*, *Deadlock* (Vienna's English Theatre) and *Miss Julie* (Theatre Royal, Haymarket). Film includes *A Cock and Bull Story* and *The Clap*. Television includes *Law and Order*, *Torn*, *Five Days*, *Poirot* and *Doctors*. Jenny was nominated for the TMA Award for Best Performance in a Play for *What Every Woman Knows*.

**David Leigh-Pemberton** | Production Manager
At the Finborough Theatre, David was Production Manager for *Events While Guarding the Bofors Gun* (2012).
Trained at The Guildhall School of Music and Drama. David is a freelance Production and Stage Manager based in London. Theatre includes *West End Bares* 2012 (Café de Paris) and *Grand Hotel* (Stratford Circus).

**Stuart Burrows** | Assistant Director
Trained at the University of Warwick and with Living Pictures. Directing includes *Accentuate The Positive* (London Palladium), *The Seven Deadly Sins* (The Roundhouse), *Band Of Brothers* (Royal Festival Hall), *The Normal Heart* (Warwick Arts Centre), *You'll Do For Now* (Cadogan Hall), *There's No Place Like Homo* (Edinburgh Festival and King's Head Theatre), *Oklahomo* (New Players Theatre and the winner of People's Choice Award at the Dublin Gay Arts Festival) and *Sweet Charity* (Brompton Oratory). Stuart was also staging director for *The Various Voices Festival* across London's South Bank Centre in 2009.

**Luke Holbrook** | Producer
Luke is Resident Assistant Producer at the Finborough Theatre where he has recently produced *Merrie England* (2012) and *Passing By* (2012). He was also General Manager for the critically-acclaimed New Writing Season (2011-12) which included *Foxfinder* and *Fog*.
Other theatre includes *London, 4 Corners: 1 Heart* (Theatre503), *A Woman Alone* (Brockley Jack Theatre) and *Ward No. 6* (Camden People's Theatre). He is also Assistant to Literary Agent Tom Erhardt at Casarotto, Ramsay and Associates Ltd.

**Production Acknowledgements**
Assistant Stage Manager | **James McLoughlin**
Production Assistant | **Caroline Mathias**
Casting Assistant | **Rose Munro**
Rehearsal Space | **The Workspace Group**
Gaelic Consultant | **Rhoda Macdonald**
Production Photography | **Richard Walker**
Press | **Finborough Theatre 07977 173135**
press@finboroughtheatre.co.uk

**Special Thanks to**
Tim Klotz
Alan Brodie Representation
Questors Theatre
Open Air Theatre, Regent's Park
Christopher Foxon
Jude Malcomson
Stephen Hunt
BAC
Guildhall School of Music and Drama

# FINBOROUGH | THEATRE

Winner – *London Theatre Reviews'* The Empty Space Peter Brook Award 2012

"An even more audacious and successful programme than ever in 2012, West London's tiny, unsubsidised Finborough Theatre is one of the best in the entire world. Its programme of new writing and obscure rediscoveries remains "jaw-droppingly good".
*Time Out / The Hospital Club*

"A disproportionately valuable component of the London theatre ecology. Its programme combines new writing and revivals, in selections intelligent and audacious."
*Financial Times*

"A blazing beacon of intelligent endeavour, nurturing new writers while finding and reviving neglected curiosities from home and abroad." *The Daily Telegraph*

Founded in 1980, the multi-award-winning Finborough Theatre presents plays and music theatre, concentrated exclusively on new writing and genuine rediscoveries from the 19th and 20th centuries. The Finborough Theatre remains unfunded by any public body, and our most significant subsidy comes from the distinguished actors, directors, designers and production team who work with us for minimal remuneration. We aim to offer a stimulating and inclusive programme, appealing to theatregoers of all ages and from a broad spectrum of the population. Behind the scenes, we continue to discover and develop a new generation of theatre makers – through our vibrant Literary team, our internship programme, our Resident Assistant Director Programme, and our partnership with the National Theatre Studio providing a bursary for Emerging Directors.

Despite remaining completely unsubsidised, the Finborough Theatre has an unparalleled track record of attracting the finest creative talent, as well as discovering new playwrights who go on to become leading voices in British theatre. Under

Artistic Director Neil McPherson, it has discovered some of the UK's most exciting new playwrights including Laura Wade, James Graham, Mike Bartlett, Sarah Grochala, Jack Thorne, Simon Vinnicombe, Alexandra Wood, Al Smith, Nicholas de Jongh and Anders Lustgarten.

Artists working at the theatre in the 1980s included Clive Barker, Rory Bremner, Nica Burns, Kathy Burke, Ken Campbell, Jane Horrocks and Claire Dowie. In the 1990s, the Finborough Theatre became known for new writing including Naomi Wallace's first play *The War Boys*; Rachel Weisz in David Farr's *Neville Southall's Washbag*; four plays by Anthony Neilson including *Penetrator* and *The Censor*, both of which transferred to the Royal Court Theatre; and new plays by Richard Bean, Lucinda Coxon, David Eldridge, Tony Marchant, Mark Ravenhill and Phil Willmott. New writing development included the premieres of modern classics such as Mark Ravenhill's *Shopping and F\*\*\*king*, Conor McPherson's *This Lime Tree Bower*, Naomi Wallace's *Slaughter City* and Martin McDonagh's *The Pillowman*.

Since 2000, new British plays have included Laura Wade's London debut *Young Emma*, commissioned for the Finborough Theatre; James Graham's *Albert's Boy* with Victor Spinetti; Sarah Grochala's *S27*; Peter Nichols' *Lingua Franca*, which transferred Off-Broadway; Anders Lustgarten's *A Day at the Racists*; Dawn King's *Foxfinder*; and West End transfers for Joy Wilkinson's *Fair*; Nicholas de Jongh's *Plague Over England*; and Jack Thorne's *Fanny and Faggot*. The late Miriam Karlin made her last stage appearance in *Many Roads to Paradise* in 2008. Many of the Finborough Theatre's new plays have been published and are on sale from our website.

UK premieres of foreign plays have included Brad Fraser's *Wolfboy*; Lanford Wilson's *Sympathetic Magic*; Larry Kramer's *The Destiny of Me*; Tennessee Williams' *Something Cloudy, Something Clear*; the English premiere of Robert McLellan's Scots language classic, *Jamie the Saxt*; and three West End transfers – Frank McGuinness' *Gates of Gold* with William Gaunt and John Bennett, Joe DiPietro's *F\*\*\*ing Men* and Craig Higginson's *Dream of the Dog* with Dame Janet Suzman.

Rediscoveries of neglected work have included the first London revivals of Rolf Hochhuth's *Soldiers* and *The Representative*; both parts of Keith Dewhurst's *Lark Rise to Candleford*; *The Women's War*, an evening of original suffragette plays; *Etta Jenks* with Clarke Peters and Daniela Nardini; Noël Coward's first play, *The Rat Trap*; Charles Wood's *Jingo* with Susannah Harker; Emlyn Williams' *Accolade* with Aden Gillett and Graham Seed; Lennox Robinson's *Drama at Inish* with Celia Imrie and Paul O'Grady; and J.B. Priestley's *Cornelius* with Alan Cox.

Music Theatre has included the new (premieres from Grant Olding, Charles Miller, Michael John LaChuisa, Adam Guettel, Andrew Lippa and Adam Gwon's *Ordinary Days* which transferred to the West End) and the old (the UK premiere of Rodgers and Hammerstein's *State Fair* which also transferred to the West End, and the acclaimed Celebrating British Music Theatre series, reviving forgotten British musicals including *Gay's The Word* by Ivor Novello with Sophie-Louise Dann, Helena Blackman and Elizabeth Seal.

The Finborough Theatre won The Stage Fringe Theatre of the Year Award in 2011, won *London Theatre Reviews'* Empty Space Peter Brook Award in 2010 and 2012, the Empty Space Peter Brook Award's Dan Crawford Pub Theatre Award in 2005 and 2008, the Empty Space Peter Brook Mark Marvin Award in 2004, four awards in the inaugural 2011 OffWestEnd Awards and swept the board with eight awards at the 2012 OffWestEnd Awards including Best Artistic Director and Best Director for the second year running. *Accolade* was named Best Fringe Show of 2011 by *Time Out*. It is the only unsubsidised theatre to be awarded the Pearson Playwriting Award bursary for writers Chris Lee in 2000, Laura Wade in 2005, James Graham in 2006, Al Smith in 2007, Anders Lustgarten in 2009, Simon Vinnicombe in 2010 and Dawn King in 2011. Three bursary holders (Laura Wade, James Graham and Anders Lustgarten) have also won the Catherine Johnson Award for Pearson Best Play.

**www.finboroughtheatre.co.uk**

The Associate Director position is supported by The National Theatre Studio's Bursary for Emerging Directors, a partnership between the National Theatre Studio and the Finborough Theatre.

The Finborough Theatre has the support of the Pearson Playwrights' Scheme. Sponsored by Pearson PLC.

The Cameron Mackintosh Resident Composer Scheme is facilitated by Mercury Musical Developments and Musical Theatre Network UK

The Finborough Theatre is a member of the Independent Theatre Council, Musical Theatre Network UK and The Earl's Court Society www.earlscourtsociety.org.uk

**Mailing**
Email admin@finboroughtheatre.co.uk or give your details to our Box Office staff to join our free email list. If you would like to be sent a free season leaflet every three months, just include your postal address and postcode.

**Follow Us Online**

www.facebook.com/FinboroughTheatre
www.twitter.com/finborough

**Feedback**
We welcome your comments, complaints and suggestions. Write to Finborough Theatre, 118 Finborough Road, London SW10 9ED or email us at admin@finboroughtheatre.co.uk

**Finborough Theatre T Shirts are now on sale from the Box Office, available in Small, Medium and Large: £7.00.**

## Friends

The Finborough Theatre is a registered charity. We receive no public funding, and rely solely on the support of our audiences. Please do consider supporting us by becoming a member of our Friends of the Finborough Theatre scheme. There are four categories of Friends, each offering a wide range of benefits.

Brandon Thomas Friends – Bruce Cleave. Matthew Littleford. Sean W. Swalwell. Michael Rangos. David Day.

Richard Tauber Friends – Neil Dalrymple. Richard Jackson. M. Kramer. Harry MacAuslan. Brian Smith. Mike Lewendon.

William Terriss Friends – Leo and Janet Liebster. Peter Lobl. Bhags Sharma. Thurloe and Lyndhurst LLP. Jon Sedmak. Jan Topham.

Smoking is not permitted in the auditorium and the use of cameras and recording equipment is strictly prohibited.

SOMERSAULTS

Iain Finlay Macleod

# SOMERSAULTS

OBERON BOOKS
LONDON
WWW.OBERONBOOKS.COM

First published in 2013 by Oberon Books Ltd
521 Caledonian Road, London N7 9RH
Tel: +44 (0) 20 7607 3637 / Fax: +44 (0) 20 7607 3629
e-mail: info@oberonbooks.com
www.oberonbooks.com

A catalogue record for this book is available from the British Library.

PB ISBN: 978-1-84943-508-6
E ISBN: 978-1-84943-813-1

Cover design: Adrian Parnham, D Sharon Pruitt/Katey Warran

Printed, bound and converted
by CPI Group (UK) Ltd, Croydon, CR0 4YY.

Visit www.oberonbooks.com to read more about all our books and to buy them. You will also find features, author interviews and news of any author events, and you can sign up for e-newsletters so that you're always first to hear about our new releases.

# Characters

JAMES
In his thirties. From the Isle of Lewis in
Scotland. Now lives in London.

ALISON
Married to James. From Cambridge.

MARK
A friend. They went to Cambrige University
together. He is from London.

SANDY
James' father.

BARRETT
A liquidator.


*The play is set in London and on the Isle of Lewis in*
*the present day.*

## ONE

*A man sits higgledy-piggledy on a sofa, it looks like a student flat, but the man is too old to be a student. JAMES. He plays a computer game, a shoot 'em up.*

*This is what he does. The sofa has grown on him, reflects the shape of his back like a shell.*

*He fills a glass with beer and knocks it back.*

*He looks at the screen again. He stops. Tilts his head.*

*He puts down the joystick.*

*He all-fours across the floor and looks at the screen. His eye is an inch from it.*

*He sits back down.*

JAMES: Fucking. Eureka.

## TWO

*JAMES' house in Hampstead, London. It is beautiful. All the objects in it are perfect. JAMES and MARK were friends in University. They have just re-connected.*

MARK: Wow.

JAMES: Call of Duty. Grand Theft Auto. Did all of them. Paid for this. All of this.

MARK: That's something.

*Pause.*

JAMES: Facebook is amazing, isn't it.

MARK: It is. It's amazing.

JAMES: How long's it been?

MARK: It's been like. When were we in Uni?

JAMES: Fifteen years ago.

MARK: From Cambridge. To here. It's like a time machine.

JAMES: Well. You popped up.

MARK: You popped up as well.

*Pause.*

JAMES: I love eBay.

MARK: Me too. I use it a lot.

JAMES: Maybe it'll be our Beatles moment. Like. Our generation did that. That's what people will say.

MARK: Do people say that?

JAMES: Some people do. I heard one person say it.

    *Pause.*

    I extrapolated.

    *Pause.*

MARK: Always used to think that was a funny word. It reminds me of 'strap-on'. I like these words. Inculcated. Extirpated.

JAMES: Is that a word?

MARK: Flagellated.

JAMES: Excommunicated.

MARK: That's a good one.

JAMES: Not so good if you're a priest.

MARK: Yes.

    *Pause.*

JAMES: How's work? Any projects?

MARK: I don't really work. I don't have to.

JAMES: I got married.

MARK: I didn't.

JAMES: I married Alison.

MARK: Alison… Alison from uni, Alison?

JAMES: Yes.

MARK: Wow. Huh. Alison.

JAMES: Yeah.

MARK: Is she still a hotty?

JAMES: She's my wife, like.

MARK: Ah.

Do you feel the same age? I do. I think it's because no really big events have happened in my life to divide me from that age. So I feel that's what I am. But there's an invisible screen between me and that age that I can never cross. One day I'm going to have to accept that my youth has gone.

*Pause.*

Well. This looks very pleasant. Nice…aspect.

JAMES: It is.

MARK: Hampstead. I love Hampstead. I used to have a flat here. And I sold it. For a loss. Imagine that.

JAMES: I've done up the basement.

MARK: Really? I'd like to see that. I should have done up the basement. That's what I should have done.

JAMES: We've extended in every way possible. I can show you? I've got a little gamesroom as well.

MARK: Lovely.

## THREE

*JAMES and MARK are pissed. They have regressed to their young selves. 'Roxanne' by The Police.*

MARK: Alright. Alright. You have to drink when he/

JAMES: Sting.

MARK: When Sting sings either Roxanne. Or red light. Simple. Simplicity is the...meat of...right.

*They play the game. They dance. They drink like troopers. They dance. They lie on the floor.*

*ALISON comes in. She doesn't speak.*

MARK: It's...

JAMES: Ali. Alison.

*Pause. To ALISON...*

If you play a Country and Western song backwards, do you get your car, house and wife back.

*JAMES and MARK burst into laughter, that kind of drunken laughter where someone can't breathe but nobody else is sure what's so funny.*

*ALISON leaves the room.*

*JAMES gets up and staggers out.*

JAMES: I need to vomit.

*MARK is alone in the room. He dances.*

## FOUR

*A bar. London. A scene from JAMES' and ALISON's courting.*

*JAMES is young. He is well-dressed. He is trying to learn to have money.*

JAMES: Yes. It came to me one day. When I was playing a computer game. There were all these hoardings which were blank. Or they'd made up company names and put up false adverts. Like Gad instead of Gap.

And I thought. There's a lot of people watching these games. What if I sell that advertising space to real companies.

And that's what I did.

ALISON: Very clever.

JAMES: You know when you see in these old films. An oil gusher. That's what it was like. For years you wonder where it was hiding. And then when it starts. Daniel Day-Lewis, right.

Red fucking Adair.

ALISON: Didn't he put *out* fires?

JAMES: I guess.

JAMES: Is it still gushing?

JAMES: I've taken my money and ran. I've got enough. I don't know if it's gushing for someone else.

ALISON: That's wise. What do you do now?

JAMES: I improve myself. Sometimes I do nothing.

*Pause.*

JAMES: I only eat twice a day.

ALISON: I've never seen on a gravestone – he was rich. It's good you didn't carry on once you had enough. You must be pretty well off.

*Pause.*

JAMES: It's nice to see you again.

ALISON: You too.

## FIVE

*JAMES and ALISON's house in Hampstead. MARK is there too, they are entertaining him. They are merry.*

MARK: Really?

JAMES: Yes.

ALISON: Don't do your Gaelic thing. Please don't start him on this.

MARK: You're having a laugh.

JAMES: It's completely kosher. Here's another one. Seadh gu dearbh. Is that right. Shag a giraffe.

27

MARK: Shag a giraffe?

JAMES: I am far away. Tha mi fad as.

MARK: Hammy fat arse.

ALISON: Don't look at me when you say that.

JAMES: Drink that. Òl siud.

MARK: All shit!

JAMES: That'll do. Fòghnaidh siud.

MARK: Phoney shit.

JAMES: Around the world. Feadh an t-saoghail.

MARK: Fucking what?

JAMES: Feadh an t-saoghail.

MARK: Fucking hell. How do I say, 'I've got a monstrously large cock?'

JAMES: Tha bod uilebheisteach agam.

MARK: Got it. Handy to know in a range of languages.

*ALISON rolls her eyes.*

MARK: Right…right…I've got a song here we go.

ALISON: Singing now is it.

MARK: One lesson. Listen to this. I did it my way. In the Gaelic Club style.
Da dum da dum Fucking hell
Phoney siud
da da da Shag a giraffe
Tha bod uilebheisteach agam.

*(Around the world*
*that'll do*
*it's true*
*I have a monstrous cock.)*

JAMES: That's the oral tradition in action.

MARK: Oral tradition!

*Laughing and drunk, JAMES goes into the kitchen to get more wine.*

MARK: *(To ALISON.)* You're lovely. I've forgotten how lovely you are.

*The air grows thick between them.*

MARK: We should have a coffee sometime.

*His statement is loaded.*

ALISON: Behave yourself.

*JAMES comes back into the room with a new bottle of wine and a corkscrew. He trips on a rug and goes for a flyer. He does a somersault. He turns, looks as if he's left something behind him.*

*JAMES' world slips.*

*A man walks from one side of the room to the other. His name is BARRETT. The others do not notice him, they continue laughing. The man looks at the books, the CD collection, a piece of art on the wall.*

*He straightens the painting and leaves.*

## SIX

*MARK and JAMES.*

JAMES: In the beginning was the word. And all that.

I've been racking my brains for it.

MARK: What.

JAMES: The Gaelic for somersault.

MARK: I just don't see what you're worried about.

JAMES: It's gone. Like that. Just like that.

MARK: Well look in a dictionary.

JAMES: No.

It just comes to me. No problem. In English. Somersault.

MARK: I just don't see. Why this is. A problem. You never speak Gaelic anyway. There's no one around you that speaks it. You said you'd never leave London. You've got a great life.

You're young. Relatively young. You've got your health, I think, or at least you look alright. You've got a nice wife.

JAMES: Ah.

*Pause.*

MARK: What do you mean, ah.

JAMES: Eh?

MARK: You said ah.

JAMES: It was an interjection. A simple interjection.

MARK: It was loaded.

JAMES: I don't want to talk about it just now.

MARK: Does Alison know about the ah?

JAMES: Mark.

MARK: James.

*Pause.*

MARK: All I'm saying is that. In the name of God Almighty and all that's holy on this earth. Why not just say somersault.

JAMES: My father has cancer.


## SEVEN

*Isle of Lewis. SANDY is JAMES' father.*

SANDY: Deagh thuras? *(Good trip?)*

JAMES: Math gu leòr. *(Good enough.)*

SANDY: Daor. *(Expensive.)*

JAMES: Trì cheud not à Glaschu. *(Three hundred pounds from Glasgow.)*

SANDY: Tha thu an-seo airson… *(You're here for…)*

JAMES: An deireadh seachdainn. Ach tha mi fuireach ann an taigh-òsta ann an Steòrnabhagh. *(The weekend. But I'm staying in a B&B. In Stornoway.)*

*Pause.*

JAMES: Bha mi duilich cluintinn. *(I was sorry to hear.)*

SANDY: Aye. Aillse na croich. *(Aye. Bloody cancer.)*

*SANDY pours a dram.*

SANDY: Dram?

JAMES: Faod thu bhith ag òl uisge-beatha? *(Are you allowed to drink whisky?)*

SANDY: Faodaidh mi dèanamh mar a thogras mi. *(I'm allowed to do whatever I like.)*

JAMES: Nach dèan e tinn thu? *(Won't it make you sick?)*

*SANDY laughs.*

SANDY: Tinn. Nach eil mi tinn. Slàinte *(Sick. I am sick. Cheers.)*

*Pause.*

Ach uill, sin mar a tha. Dè tha thu ris na làithean-sa? *(Ach well, that's how it is. What are you up to these days?)*

JAMES: Ach. *(JAMES notices the sheep are gone from the field.)* Trobhad seo, dè rinn thu le na caoraich? *(Ach. Here, where are the sheep?)*

SANDY: Dh'ith mi iad. *(I ate them.)*

JAMES: Dè rinn thu leotha? *(What did you do with them?)*

SANDY: Och, fhuair mi riods iad. Cha d'fhuair mi mòran air an son. *(Och, I got rid of them. Didn't get much for them.)*

JAMES: Carson? Bha gaol agads' air na diabhail chaoraich sin. *(Why? You loved these bloody sheep.)*

SANDY: Cus obair annta. *(They were too much work.)*

JAMES: B'urrainn dhuinn cìobair fhaighinn. *(We could get a shepherd.)*

SANDY: Cìobair. *(Shepherd.)*

JAMES: Nach urrainn dhut sin a dhèanamh. *(You can do that, can't you.)*

SANDY: Cìobair. *(Shepherd.)*

'Se an Tighearna fhèin is buachaille dhomh. Aon latha tha thu a' cluich am measg nan gocan feòir. An ath latha tha na casan agad air an dèanamh a-mach à iarann.

*(The Lord's my Shepherd. One day you're playing in the corn stooks. The next your legs are made of cast iron.)*

JAMES: Fhios agad nuair a bhitheas thu…fios agad am facal… *(You know when you…you know the word…)*

SANDY: Airson? *(For?)*

JAMES: Somersault. Ann am Beurla. Dè Ghàidhlig a th'air. *(Somersault. In English. What's the Gaelic for it.)*

SANDY: A' Ghàidhlig airson somersault? Tha cho fada bho rinn mi fear. *(The Gaelic for somersault? It's so long since I've done one.)*

*SANDY stands and looks out of the window.*

Bha latha ann bhithinn gan dèanamh gu math tric.

Chan eil fhios agam. *(There was a day I used to do them all the time. I don't know.)*

Seo. Sin faclair. *(Here. There's a dictionary.)*

*He gives the dictionary to SEUMAS.*

Cuiridh mis' air an coire. *(I'll put the kettle on.)*

*He leaves the room. SEUMAS is left holding the dictionary, looking at it.*

JAMES: Fuck sake.

## EIGHT

*MARK's flat. London. JAMES somersaults.*

JAMES: I have a space. Where the word was. I have the picture in my head. I can smell the hay and my father picking me up and turning head over and up again and falling into that deep cushion of fresh raked hay. The sun up and bent figures in the field.

MARK: Well. You won't need to be in a field again. Will you.

JAMES: I don't know why I'm worried about this word.

When my life is winnowing before my eyes.

A fucking halibut of doom waving like a giant cock in front of my face.

MARK: Are you alright?

JAMES: Turns out I'm not so clever. As I thought I was.

## NINE

*JAMES' flat in London. BARRETT is with JAMES. He is the liquidator that has been attached to JAMES' bankruptcy.*

BARRETT: Yes, sir. We leave you the necessities of life.

JAMES: Which are.

BARRETT: Do you really want me to relate them?

JAMES: Yes.

BARRETT: I'll leave a list. How about that.

JAMES: Tell me one. Then.

BARRETT: Saucepans. We leave you saucepans. But. Looking on the bright side. We also leave your resourcefulness. And your spirit. And your arms and legs.

JAMES: What atrophy.

BARRETT: Look at it this way. Like a great cleaning fire which has freed you from many things.

JAMES: Many things. Such as?

BARRETT: You will have to re-evaluate your materialistic tendencies.

JAMES: I have materialistic tendencies?

BARRETT: Evidently. Obviously. I've been handling your proclivities. Do you really need a car like that?

JAMES: I did.

BARRETT: Why.

JAMES: The car increased what I earned.

BARRETT: Your situation hints to the contrary.

*Pause.*

BARRETT: Is your wife leaving you?

JAMES: That's private.

BARRETT: I'm afraid nothing is private anymore. I know everything.

JAMES: I'm a folder. Am I. That's what I am now. One of your folders. A Manila.

BARRETT: Look on the bright side.

*Pause.*

JAMES: Well?

BARRETT: I don't know what the bright side is. You'll have to find one.

*Pause.*

But. On reflection. There are lots of people who are worse off than you.

JAMES: That's meant to make me feel better?

BARRETT: It's an effort. It's a concrete effort.

## TEN

*An Art Gallery.*

JAMES: Are you fucking kidding me?

ALISON: What.

JAMES: Dutch Masters? This is what you thought would be, this is what you think, this is a good use of a Saturday? My life is imploding. Haven't you noticed? Haven't you noticed?

ALISON: We're getting to spend time together. That's what's important.

JAMES: Have you any idea have you really/

ALISON: Can you, maybe keep it down a little.

JAMES: any idea of how uninteresting this is to me.

*Pause.*

ALISON: I was trying to find something you enjoyed to take your mind off things. You mentioned you liked German films.

JAMES: When did I say that? These are paintings. They're not even German. When did I say that?

ALISON: At the start.

JAMES: I said a lot of things at the start in the hope that incrementally they would add up in your brain to convince you I would be a good mate.

ALISON: Mate. As in. You're talking more about. Baboons. And things. Rather than a relationship.

JAMES: I'm talking about mating.

ALISON: Well…that's…fucking charming.

I am being very kind to you, James. You just don't realise it.

I think the paintings are beautiful. I think the light in Holland is beautiful.

JAMES: The light in Holland? The fucking light in Holland?

*They part to look at paintings. JAMES looks about him. All clear. He does a somersault.*

ALISON: What the hell are you doing?

JAMES: FUCKING CUNTING BOLLOCKS!


## ELEVEN

*The house. MARK and ALISON.*

MARK: How are you coping?

ALISON: Oh well. It's not easy. He's having to sell his paintings. I hated these paintings.

MARK: Are they not your paintings as well?

ALISON: He would buy these things. He wouldn't know what they were. None of them were pictures like a landscape or a haystack or even a person. Living in this house was like permanently being in a bad exhibition at the Tate. He liked the couches there. So we have couches at home like a little Tate gallery.

MARK: Like a pony-sized Pompidou Centre.

ALISON: It's what a French person would buy if they had money, were quite pretentious, but had no taste.

MARK: I like the Tate.

ALISON: I like the Tate too. Love it.

MARK: They'll probably fetch a lot of money.

ALISON: Hmm. He has this freaky little man who's attached to him/

MARK: Who?

ALISON: James, does. He looks at James like a balance sheet. His legs are fixed assets. His stomach is tax deductible. His head is a…his head is a director's loan…no…his head is a…

MARK: Jokes about accountancy maybe aren't your strong point.

ALISON: No.

*Pause.*

We were happy.

MARK: No you weren't.

Where is he now?

ALISON: Up in Lewis. Considering the lillies.

## TWELVE

*SANDY sits. JAMES comes in.*

JAMES: Càit a bheil am faclair? *(Where's the dictionary?)*

SANDY: Eh?

JAMES: Am faclair. *(The dictionary.)*

SANDY: Shad mi a-mach e. Threw it out.

JAMES: Eh.

SANDY: Shad mi a-mach na leabhraichean. Ach an aon. *(Threw out lots of books. Except one.)*

JAMES: No books. What, are you a minister now.

SANDY: I wish I were.

JAMES: Are you getting the cùram *(religion)* now.

SANDY: Nothing wrong with a policy of insurance.

JAMES: Having your cake and eating it.

SANDY: I've raised a heathen. You atheists don't want any comfort for anybody.

*Pause.*

37

I'm supposed to like everyone in the world now.

JAMES: Na sad a' chòrr a-mach. *(Don't throw anything else out.)*

SANDY: Eh.

JAMES: Na sad a' chòrr a-mach. *(Don't throw anything else out.)*

SANDY: Faodaidh tu na deisean agam fhaighinn. *(You can have my suits.)*

JAMES: You'll need your suits.

SANDY: I'll only need one where I'm going.

JAMES: Danns' an rathaid? *(A road dance?)*

*Pause.*

SANDY: Bhàsaich James Brown. Agus seall cho math 's a bha esan air dannsa. *(James Brown died. And look what a good dancer he was.)*

*Pause.*

Bu chòir dhomh bhith air fuireach ann an New Zealand. Bhiodh na leumadairean a' cluich air an t-suaile air beulaibh a' bhàta. *(I should have stayed in New Zealand. And the dolphins would always come out and play in the bow wave.)*

*He moves his hands in their shape.*

Bha craobhan eadar-dhealaichte aca an-sin. Agus eòin. Iseanan beaga breagha.

Auckland. Rotorua.Wellington. Dh'fhaodadh tu seoba fhàgail anns a' mhadainn agus gheibheadh tu fear eile an deidh lunch.

Bha cho furasta jump ship a dhèanamh.

*(They had such different trees there. And birds. Pretty little birds.*

*Auckland. Rotorua. Wellington. You could leave your job in the morning and get another one by lunch.*

*It was so easy to jump ship.)*

The funny thing is you don't feel the pain from the thing itself.

JAMES: You enjoyed Argentina as well.

SANDY: Corned beef. Chuirinn corned beef dhachaigh gu do mhàthair.

B'urrainn dhomh bhith air fuireach a-muigh ann. Bha mi anns a' Phanama Canal, a' dol a-mach gu New Zealand. Bhàsaich m'athair agus rinn mi suaip le aon dhe na balaich air bòrd bàta bha tied up ri ar cliathaich. Swapped passages. Chaidh mise air ais dhachaigh. Chaidh esan a-mach. Rinn sinn suaip air ar cuid beatha.

Chòrdadh sin rium an-dràsta.

A man, a plan, a canal. Panama.

*(Corned beef. I would send corned beef home to your mother.*

*I could have stayed out there. I was in the Panama Canal, heading out to Australia when my father died. I swapped with one of the lads on the boat beside us. Swapped passages. I went back home. He went out there. We swapped lives.*

*I'd like that just now.*

*A man, a plan, a canal. Panama.)*

*JAMES is standing behind SANDY, looking out of the window. He puts his hand on his shoulder and then gives him a hug. His father turns and hugs him back. It is the first time they have touched apart from shaking hands since he was a little boy. It is the smallest moment.*

## THIRTEEN

*JAMES and BARRETT.*

BARRETT: I just don't really see…what this has to do with me?

JAMES: There's other words. Missing. Hundreds of them.

They're in there somewhere. They need to rise to the surface. Of their own accord.

The word for the little cream flower. Cream yellow on the potato stalk. And. My father was a weaver. The name of the little shuttle…that he would put the…the iteachan…in.

BARRETT: What's that then?

JAMES: I don't know the English for it.

*JAMES smiles.*

BARRETT: I'm not really interested in any of that.

You like rock music. An excellent collection.

*He flicks through some records.*

Stones. Stones. Stones. Stones. Zep. Zep. Zappa. Clapton. Stones.

JAMES: When will this be finished?

BARRETT: In about half an hour. There won't be much left of you, then. Anything, in fact.

JAMES: Excuse me?

BARRETT: You're disappearing.

JAMES: There's no need to rub it in. I'll have plenty left. After you go back to whatever box you live in. I'll have words. We're made up of words.

BARRETT: Well. You appear to be forgetting yours.

*Pause.*

JAMES: Do you have a wife?

BARRETT: I'd rather not talk about that.

JAMES: I think you like to go to certain types of clubs.

*Pause.*

We're sort of friends now. Don't you think.

BARRATT: I would say conclusively. I think so.

JAMES: You love your job, don't you. You love taking people apart.

BARRATT: You have me all wrong. What I'm doing is saving you. I am bringing order.

JAMES: So what do I do now? I need to get home. I need to go north.

BARRETT: You'll get an allowance.

JAMES: Give it to me now.

BARRETT: That's against the rules. You have more chance of finding work here. Statistically. You must have contacts. Old friends who will help you. A network.

*Silence.*

Some friends on Facebook?

JAMES: There's nothing here for me anymore. I need to go back.

There's earth there. Black earth. I can grow things. I'll be far away from you.

I just need seeds. Rain. Light. There are still fish. I can fish.

BARRETT: With your hands, like a Famous Five book.

JAMES: I can fish. I have a bamboo rod. My father has land. I can dig.

BARRETT: This wasn't mentioned in the assets.

JAMES: It's his. You can't touch it. I can kill a sheep. I can rear and kill animals. I can put a stone on top of another stone on top of another stone and stop the wind. I can build walls. A roof. I can climb cliffs and find the seabird eggs. I can cut peats. Have you seen the moors on the island. Have you seen the sea.

BARRETT: You have soft hands.

*Pause.*

That's all very nice.

*BARRETT takes out a cheque from his top pocket. He puts it on the table.*

But I think you might have missed your window of opportunity. I'm afraid we're together in this. Till the bitter end.

JAMES: There's a summer village they used to go to. Where I can find all of these things. It's empty now. You would never find me there. You don't even know what a summer village is.

Transhumance. That's what it was for. Moving the animals to the summer grazing. The àiridh. That's what it's called. You don't even know that. Do you. You know nothing.

BARRETT: Thug mi an oidhche raoir san àirigh.

*(This is a line from a famous Gaelic song about a summer village – an 'àirigh'.)*

*BARRETT picks up the albums.*

JAMES: That's a song. That's a line from a song.

*BARRETT sings it.*

How do you know that.

Are you hiding yourself?


## FOURTEEN

*Isle of Lewis. JAMES and his father, SANDY.*

SANDY: Carson a tha thu a' faighneachd sin a-nis. *(Why are you asking me that now.)*

JAMES: Maybe it's my age. They say that you get more interested in things like this when you reach a certain age.

SANDY: It's called an t-Slugaid.

JAMES: That's a placename.

SANDY: That's a place and that's its name.

*Pause.*

What's the point in learning a little bit here. A little bit there. Like a magpie. Little shiny thing.

JAMES: What's that shieling on the moor called?

SANDY: Filiscleitir. You may as well be picking pebbles off a beach.

JAMES: I was wondering if you had your old loom?

SANDY: Mo bheairt? Carson a bha thu wondering that? *(Why were you wondering that?)*

JAMES: Just been thinking about it. It'd be nice to see it working again.

SANDY: Working again? Who's going to do that? Chan eil mise dol a dhèanamh sin. *(I'm not going to do that.)*

JAMES: There must be cuideigin. *(someone.)*

SANDY: No. Well. Couple of old guys. You'll have to be quick. If they want to do it at all.

JAMES: Where is it?

SANDY: Anns an t-sabhal. *(In the barn.)*

JAMES: Is it well stored?

SANDY: 'S bheag mo dhiù. *(Little do I care.)*

JAMES: I do.

SANDY: The happiest day of my life was when I took it apart. Inneal na croich. *(Hellish machine.)*

JAMES: It's important. It's a beautiful old… 's ann a Yorkshire a bha e. Hattersley. It was like proper a proper thing.

*Pause.*

JAMES: Dè mar a tha an treatment? *(How is the treatment going?)*

SANDY: Dìreach diabhalt. Tha mi ag iarraidh bàsachadh. *(Hellish. I want to die.)*

JAMES: Na can sin. *(Don't say that.)*

SANDY: Carson. Tha e fior. *(Why. It's true.)*

*Pause.*

Nobody asks old people for advice. Have you noticed.

I've never understood that.

I'm going to give you some comhairle. *(advice.)*

I remember going to the doctor years ago. I said to him, I'm worried about my cholesterol. He looked at me and said 'what's an old amadan *(idiot)* like you doing worrying about your cholesterol.' And I skipped down the street. That's some advice. Don't take it all too seriously.

As for vanity. My life improved a lot when I decided just to wear elasticated trousers. These are things to remember later in life, Seumas.

*Pause.*

You don't need to be here. You go and live your own life.

*Pause.*

Tha mi airson gum bi e luath. *(I want it to be quick.)* Not like this. I thought of going out ann am bàta. *(on a boat.)* Stoirm. In a storm. Slipping down le mo ghàirdeanan paisgte. *(with my arms crossed.)* To the bottom. Grunnd. Fairge. Tonn. Stuagh. Cìrean. Suaile. *(Different names for waves.)* Going out standing up. But we cling on. We cling on. The doctors have ways now. They can stretch out your life on next to nothing.

*Pause.*

I don't want to be the last. The last of the Mohicans. Chòrd am fiolm sin rium. *(Enjoyed that film.)*

*Pause.*

What's wrong?

Are you crying.

Ah. Dhuine bhochd. Sguir a rànail. *(Jesus. Stop crying.)*

You always used to cry when you were little.

Siuthad, sguir. Cùm agad fhèin e. *(Stop it. Keep it to yourself.)*

JAMES: Duilich.

Sorry.

SANDY: Comes to us all. Why should I be any different.

JAMES: You talk about it like…you talk like…

SANDY: What.

JAMES: Chan eil càil. *(Nothing.)*

SANDY: Supposed to be brightening me up. How's London?

JAMES: Tha mi bankrupt. Chaill mi an taigh. *(I'm bankrupt. I lost the house.)*

SANDY: Ach well. What's the worst that can happen.

JAMES: Alison left me.

SANDY: She was a nice woman.

*Pause.*

JAMES: I was thinking I could maybe move in here for a while.

I've got so much to learn.

I'm trying to remember some words. Will you help me?

SANDY: I'm a bit busy.

*Pause.*

SANDY: I'm just joking. Joking. Aidh. *(Aye.)*

JAMES: I'll run them by you later.

SANDY: Aidh.

*Pause.*

Well, that was uabhasach snog. *(nice.)* Passing the time. Aidh aidh.

## FIFTEEN

*SANDY passes away.*

*JAMES stands in the barn. He is surrounded by pieces of loom.*

*Pieces of useless old tweed. Cast iron circles. Discarded cogs. Other objects and tools which he had names for earlier.*

*He does not know where to start putting it together. It is now too late.*

*He picks up a croman (a small hoe-like tool). The handle is holed with woodworm.*

*A speal (a scyth). Rust.*

*JAMES scyths the air.*

## SIXTEEN

*MARK and JAMES.*

MARK: I have to go out.

JAMES: I'm trying to remember the word for… *(To himself, trying to talk himself into remembering.)* …ten men lift the bier. The closest relatives walk before and after it, holding a velvet rope. Everyone takes a turn…you walk ten paces and swap. Walk ten paces and swap.

And then the…

And then the…

*He holds a handful of soil. The word he has forgotten is 'dust' – the Gaelic word for the remains.*

MARK: And.

JAMES: He was going back out for good, when he swapped passages in the Panama Canal. To come back home when his father died.

I'm sure I had a word for…

MARK: What?

JAMES: You know how some people say that they spoke a language until they were five. Totally fluent. And now, now that they're older, it's forgotten. I had a friend who was brought up in Malaysia who spoke Malay until he was five and then he left and then he forgot it. But it must be there somewhere. Imprinted.

MARK: Why? Why would it be.

JAMES: Because of the time it happened. That young. And if something was to trigger it, it would all flood back. That's what I feel like just now. That there's a space. That I need a trigger.

MARK: Tell me another word.

*Pause.*

JAMES: I can't think of any.

MARK: It's the stress of the funeral.

JAMES: No no no no. I don't feel good. It doesn't feel good. There's something happening. Does my face look OK?

MARK: They have websites where you can self-diagnose.

JAMES: I need to loosen off.

*He shakes his arms out. BARRETT comes in.*

MARK: It's not really a good time.

BARRETT: He looks peaky.

MARK: His father has just died.

BARRETT: Oh? I have smelling salts should we need them. I always carry them.

JAMES: It's gone. It's really gone.

BARRETT: What has?

JAMES: I spoke something else.

*A pause. Then BARRETT laughs.*

BARRETT: I think you've slipped between the pages a little bit, my friend. Have a seat. You still have chairs. A necessity of life. New chairs. New inventory. What are these things?

*He points to the loom.*

JAMES: They are PARTS of a FUCKING LOOM you little troich. *(troll.)*

MARK: He's emotional.

BARRETT: He's a live one. They don't look like they have any value. We'll discount them. Along with all these other objects. Quite a little collector, aren't we.

JAMES: I'll give you… I'll give you value… I'll carve you up like a trifle and put little stickers on your little legs and your eyes and your fingers and I'll put little price tags on them/

MARK: I think you're aggravating him.

BARRATT: You don't carve a trifle. You serve a trifle.

JAMES: And then I'll sell you on eBay and you'll disappear, we'll see about your value then. Look. Look at my leg. What value does this have. What about in here? My head. What about this. What about my voice. What about my spirit. Left-hand column. Left-hand column. My aggression. My love. My will. My toes.

BARRETT: What you don't seem to understand is. I'm here to be a friend for you for the whole process.

JAMES: I want to go home. To my father's house. To my mother's house.

BARRETT: Your parents are gone. The house is gone. Your mother is gone. Your father is gone. Your wife is gone. Your money is gone. Your furniture is gone. Your words have gone. The silhouette of you against the sea as a young boy that your father remembers is gone. Your youth is gone. Your life is gone. It's all gone.

JAMES: No. I can go home. When I want.

BARRATT: It's gone.

JAMES: Wait. I can…just wait.

*JAMES tries to recreate the world around him.*

Isle of Lewis. Interior. House. Daytime. A man comes into a room. He is about thirty. Tall. Or maybe small. The room is in the house he was brought up in. There is a small hole in one of the walls. The man goes over and looks in the break and finds leaves of a Bible and written on one of the many layers of wallpaper – his father's name and a date, 1952.

The man sits on the floor. Since his father has died the room is full of things he remembers. A picture of his grandfather when he was a young man in Canada. There is the picture of a ship – The Rangitoto – on which his father took passage to New Zealand. There is a shuttle. Five shuttles waiting to be used in a loom, still brand new in their paper. A spàl. *(A shuttle.)*

Spàl.

Sin e. Sin a t-ainm a th'air. *(That's its name.)*

Spàl.

The man looks at the object agus ann am priobadh na sùla tha e a' cuimhneachadh air na facail bàrr-gùc am flùr air buntàta agus spàl agus deamhais airson bearradh nan caorach agus croman agus far a bheil an tobair air a' mhòintich faisg air na h-àirighean agus tairsgear air a bhogadh ann an uisge an latha mus tèid a chleachdadh, calcas, am broinn, gàrradh, stèidheadh, togail, tarraing agus/

*(The man looks at the object and in the blink of an eye he remembers the words the flower on the potato stalk and the shuttle and hand shears and the little hoe and where the well is on the moor near the summer village and the cutting iron in water the day before being used, calcas, the inside of the peat bank, lifting the peats, taking home the peats and/)*

BARRETT: James. I'm sorry. It really all has to go. You'll hardly feel a thing. I don't want to have to reduce you to nothing. But sometimes that's just what happens.

Even now, James. You've got too much.

You're an invention. A character gradually being reduced to nothing. That's what happened to me. And look how things worked out for me. Couldn't be better. I let all these things go. And now I don't bother anybody and sometimes I even get to do what I like.

You've got to let go or else it'll only get worse. Look.

*MARK and ALISON make love. JAMES watches them.*

JAMES: Why are you doing this?

MARK: I told you I was going out. You kept on asking.

ALISON: Shut the door, James. I'm busy.

MARK: Make us a cup of tea, love.

JAMES: A cup of tea! A fucking cup of tea!

BARRETT: Hope. Hope will destroy you.

ALISON: Them's the breaks.

MARK: C'est la vie.

BARRETT: James/

JAMES: My name's Seumas. That's what my father called me and it's his choice.

BARRETT: All walls disappear for him. There are no more walls in the world. The object has gone. Signifier signified as dust. The word has gone. It is as if it never existed.

See. That wasn't so bad. Was it. Oop. There goes something else. His childhood. But that's fine. It was conventional and won't be missed, apart from the fact that for six months of his life he would construct sentences using bits of two languages. What two languages, well, that doesn't really matter.

Look at this map of the village. This map was originally
littered with names. The places still exist. Fair enough.
But if the people aren't there who need to use markers to
construct a spatial frame of reference. Well, what's the use.
Bye bye.

James is looking pretty down now. It almost feels cruel to
take what's left away but we know it's for the best. He'll
be a new man after it. Totally refreshed. Unblemished.
Untouchable.

You're hiding it from me. Tell me.

JAMES: I don't know what you're talking about.

BARRETT: I want it.

*He remembers.*

BARRETT: You're hiding a word. Just say it.

*BARRETT leaves.*


## SEVENTEEN

*THE OTHER ACTORS ARE SEATED IN THE AUDIENCE.*

*THE ACTOR PLAYING JAMES SITS DOWN AND STARTS TO
TALK.*

Am I sad that my language is dying.

Yes I am.

It does sometimes make me very low. That all these things
I know are on such light ground, such faint anchors.

Words are released all the time and each death in the
village is felt, like the death of a part of us all, we are
weakened. I feel the edges of the light move in and wonder
if one day there will only be me, or someone like me,
carrying words for the world which no one else knows.
Like car a' mhuiltein, the Gaelic word for somersault.

I have tried the other way, to ignore it, to work on a part of
me which is not disappearing.

You hope it continues without you. Expect it to. Then one day, you cannot help it. You turn and the world you knew is no longer there.

Would it be the same if it was a block of flats in Glasgow, London, Toronto, Paris, that these people are coming and going.

That people came and went. That words came and went.

I don't know.

Especially when you realise the world is change, anyway.

Constant creation and death. Why should it matter to us. If a few words then a few more and then a language just go.


## EIGHTEEN

*THE ACTOR PLAYING ALISON.*

Do you think in Gaelic.

Do you dream in Gaelic.

Are the questions that come and I reply, yes of course and they look at you and they hear your answer but they do not think it can be real because it is something which can't be imagined. Just as I cannot imagine what it must be like to think what they think.

Can you think in two languages at the same time?

And why would you want to when English does everything. I can buy newspapers in English and talk to people in Singapore in English and I can order a burger in Dubai in English.

It is a miracle that small things still survive. It must be hard to eradicate a language. It must go deep. Or else why is it still here. Even when people have tried to beat it out of people.

In school, not so long ago. The teacher would give a paddle to a child, who gave it to the first child they heard speaking Gaelic, who gave it to the next child speaking Gaelic and the child with the paddle at the end of the day was beaten with it.

All my schooling was in English. So I cannot write Gaelic properly. And so it goes.

You talk to a schoolchild now and they have lots of words you've never heard of. They have learnt different numbers to you. They count in tens. You count in twenties.

Not so long ago it was still illegal to have your name in Gaelic on your gravestone.

## NINETEEN

*THE ACTOR PLAYING MARK.*

I like English people. I like people from Fife. I like people from Rio de Janeiro. But I'm sure you'll still find right fuckers in their midst, real horrible people, but generally one makes an effort to like people. It doesn't bother me if Brazilians speak Portugese. On a night out, drinking Madeira.

This is what happens to me, on average, once a year. We go out sometimes there's a room full of people and one person only speaks English so we speak English so that they feel at home and so that we're not being rude like the fucking Gaels that we are. Would a Welsh person do this? No. Welsh people who speak Welsh don't give a fuck if they appear rude. And that's why there's so many of them.

Then you get drunk and a few words slip out. 'Please don't speak that language, it's rude.' Just like that. Stop speaking that language. Do you say that to chatting German people? This is specifically Scottish people who do this. Never someone English. I saw it on Facebook just last week. Facebook! Someone from Stornoway.

Living in Scotland speaking Gaelic, I get the strong impression that we are resented and that people find us in some strange way, offensive. That really it would be much nicer if we just went away. Am I wrong?

Is it historical? There is a saying in Gaelic. Mì-rùn mòr nan Gall. 'The great ill will of the Lowlander'. So someone else has felt it.

Is it because you think people are talking about you when they switch to another language? Please! Enough about you already! It's just good fun speaking Gaelic. It's natural. It's our mother tongue. It is in the nature of a frog to be a frog. It's just something that we do. Like Brazilians speak Portugese. And English people speak English.

There's enough English in your life. You get enough. The whole fucking universe is geared to your linguistic pleasure. My English is better than the Queen's. I bet she misses the odd apostrophe. Me? Never. The cat sat on the fucking mat!

Maybe it might be good for you if you learnt how to say hello in another language or two. Have you thought about that? Guten Tag, you rude little fucker.

Sorry. That's not very polite. I do apologise.

You've got to realise I can't be reasoned with. That this is an emotional thing.


## TWENTY

*THE ACTOR PLAYING SANDY.*

You know, what is the point of Gaelic anyway.

What can you do in it that you can't do in English.

What relevance, really, does it have for someone from Glasgow. From Govan, say.

Or from Stornoway. Sometimes.

They never, ever spoke Gaelic in Aberdeen.

Will it improve their lives?

The answer is no.

And yet we spend all this money on it.

Millions of pounds!

I said it!

Millions of pounds on television programmes that only some people can watch.

If you did it in English everyone could watch.

Apart from the people who only spoke Punjabi.

And there's *still* more of them than fucking Gaelic speakers.

It makes me so angry.

Who the *fuck* needs Thomas the *fucking* Tank Engine in Gaelic?

## TWENTY-ONE

I gave up learning Gaelic. It's too difficult and I'll always be labelled a learner.

It's more useful to learn French or German. I'm learning some Mandarin, actually. A billion speakers!

## TWENTY-TWO

There are surprisingly few loan words between Gaelic and Scots, even though they have lived side by side for so long. Maybe muckle. In Gaelic we say muiceal. For something big. Gansey. Geansaidh. Bròg. Brogue.

You can say things like. Scunnered. High heijin. Fanny baws. Fu's a fish. I wis like 'at. Gonnae no. Shneister (although I think my friend made this word up. He says it is from Ayrshire and means a small snack that you have with a cup of tea). Wee, sleekit, cow'rin, tim'rous beastie, O, what a panic's in thy breastie. Fit like? Chavving awa. Thrawn. Gleikit. Hoose! Foo's yer doos? Bairns. That's what they say in Swedish as well. Bairns. What if these words just disappeared.

## TWENTY-THREE

*Words from Gaelic borrowed into English.*

Smashing – From 's math sin. That's good.

Slogan – from sluagh ghairm. A calling to arms.

Clan – Clann. Children.

Whisky. Uisge-beatha! The water of life.

*Words borrowed from English into Gaelic.*

Helicopter

Washing machine

International Space Station

Porn. Only joking.

*Gaelic words which sound funny in English.*

Fanaidh mi siud aig a' phartaidh, òl siud, shag a giraffe.

*English words which sound funny in Gaelic.*

Peach. Fanny.

## TWENTY-FOUR

There are words that I only know the Gaelic for.

Bàrr-gùc. The flower that comes on a potato stalk. It's a beautiful white, creamy flower and there's yellow as well.

Calcas. The stringy stuff you get in peat which sticks on your peat cutting iron.

Uinneag an latha – the small frame of day that's left in the sky when the night is almost here.

There are of course words which I have borrowed from English, like helicopter washing machine and stuff like that.

But I don't know the word in English for a moon which isn't high in the sky. 'Gealach cùl nan gàrraidhean'. And you don't have fifty words for the sea.

I made that last bit up.

## TWENTY-FIVE

If you were to go home tonight and the language that your mother spoke, imagine it was English, the language whose sound you heard first when you came into this world, that ordered the world for you, if that language was dying. How would you feel. If all of it was obliterated. If it was all silence.

If you could hear the gradual winnowing and feel the approaching death.

## TWENTY-SIX

I sometimes wonder what it would be like to be the last speaker of a language. There are a number of people in the world who are in this situation.

I imagine sitting by myself by a fire and thinking and chuckling.

All your jokes would be private jokes.

All your secrets would go to the grave with you.

Because they would be indecipherable to anyone else alive.

I'd make tea for a documentary crew that came to visit me and they would look at old tools that people before me used to winnow the grain, to dig the soil. And I'd talk romantically about these things even though digging and things like that isn't in the least romantic when you are doing it. Not really. Maybe if you are tending a rose. Not if you have a sore back. The tools have a little woodworm now and would break.

They would record me and I would sit in a library. I would get a copy of it for my archives.

And I would sit and pretend I was in *Krapp's Last Tape* by Samuel Beckett and listen to words and record myself listening to words and listen to my young self and comment on it and record that, then I would listen to a song that no one else in the world understands anymore and I would feel all-powerful as well as insignificant. And I would feel that if I could listen enough and record enough I could get it all back.

And I would take all these tapes and play them and I would be surrounded by voices, it would be like being at a fank, in the pub, at a concert, having a meal with friends. I would drink a whisky and enjoy that. Until the final voice left was the one singing and the sound of it would fill the room.

*The voice of a young child talks about somersaulting. We see the word in the air.*

*End.*